THE MOUNTAIN BEHIND THE HOUSE

Also by Kobus Moolman

All and Everything (uHlanga Press, 2019)

The Swimming Lesson and Other Stories (UKZN Press, 2017)

A Book of Rooms (Deep South, 2014)

Left Over (Dye Hard Press, 2013)

Light and After (Deep South, 2010)

Anatomy (Caversham Press, 2008)

Separating the Seas (UKZN Press, 2007)

Blind Voices: A Collection of Radio Plays (Botsotso Publishers, 2007)

Full Circle (Dye Hard Press, 2007)

Feet of the Sky (Brevitas Press, 2003)

Time like Stone (UKZN Press, 2000)

THE MOUNTAIN BEHIND THE HOUSE

by

Kobus Moolman

People! Read Poetry

THE MOUNTAIN BEHIND THE HOUSE

Dryad Press (Pty) Ltd
Postnet Suite 281, Private Bag X16 Constantia, 7848,
Cape Town, South Africa
www.dryadpress.co.za
business@dryadpress.co.za

Cover design and typography: Stephen Symons
Author photograph: Peter Buss
Editor: Michèle Betty
Copy Editor: Helena Janisch

Set in 9.5/14pt Palatino Linotype
Printed and bound by Digital Action (Pty) Ltd

First published in Cape Town by Dryad Press (Pty) Ltd, 2020

Visit www.dryadpress.co.za to read more about all our books and to buy them.
You will also find features, links to author interviews and news of author
events. Follow our social media platforms on Instagram and Facebook to be
the first to hear about our new releases.

ISBN 978-1-990961-97-7

Dryad Press is supported by the Government of South Africa through the
National Arts Council of South Africa (an Agency of the Department of Arts &
Culture), whose assistance is gratefully acknowledged.

for Julia

soli deo gloria

CONTENTS

I Mountain

II Here

III There

IV Mother

V Everywhere

VI Bone

VII Nowhere

VIII Aubade

There is a moment, in the mountains, when the first light does not so much fill the sky as empty it still further, the day itself initiated by a vacuum opening in the east.

– Stephen Watson, *A Writer's Diary*

In essence, the poet has only one theme: his live body.

– George Seferis, *A Poet's Journal: Days of 1945–1951*

I

Mountain

New House

There is no mountain at the front of the new house.

There are only birds and thin fever trees.

There are only small stones and the shouts of children.

At the back of the new house is where the mountain lives.

The mountain with its hard high forehead.

The mountain with its infinite number of steps into the clouds.

At the back of the new house there is the mountain.

And small plants that survive only on air.

And yellow fish that change behind the curtain of the wind.

II

Here

I Am That Stone

I am that stone.

      Red mountain in the morning.

I am that stone that sits.

      Sharp static of cicadas.

I am that stone that sits still.

      Sky between wind and rock.

I am that stone that burns silently.

Blue Door

All is still.
      Sky bangs a blue
door in the face
of burning rock.

      Barely birds move,
small high stones through
air dry as sunlight.

      I am shadow
sheltered in the stoop
of a small tree.

I am salt
      that tastes of seeing.
Old bone cracked beneath
the weight of insects.

Biedouw Valley

Tireless, all day the wind has been
building a nest in the acacia tree:
sticks thin as insects, desiccated
white bone propping up
the sharpness of cicadas; dry bushes
scratch the soft ceiling of an old sky.
  But held together by dust,
the tree's secret cannot be separated
from the gulf that lies between
every separate thing, the way holes
hold together old nets, where flies
breed, rotting the air.

Riebeek Valley Dawn

Rooster fetches small birds
    from the dark.

Heavy thorn branches drag
    their sound over stones.

Wind brings the trees
    to climax again and again.

Dawn melts a film of blue
    around the top of the sky.

Never the Same

Sky stays never
the same. Clouds
come in and go out
of different doors.
There are deep footprints
where the mountain
crosses the threshold
of the wind. A crack
in the wall lets
the other side in.
The floor is sprung.
Old sagging beams
keep the birds in the air.

Harvest

An old tractor trundles by,
pulling two wagons piled
high with grapes.

Little sparrows build
their scrappy nests in the fork
of a fever tree.

The driver of the tractor
goes up and down all day long
between the vineyards

and the big processing plant.
A lone turtle dove
calls and calls in the heat.

Little Girl

Her grandmother sits on the green plastic chair with
the broken back.

Her mother sits on an upturned Black Label crate.

Her sister sits and sleeps on her mother's lap.

Her auntie (on her mother's side) sits on the stump used for
chopping wood and for chopping off the heads of chickens.

Her mother's disabled cousin sits in her wheelchair, the one
with the stupid front wheel.

Her father hasn't been seen for three years, since he left
to find work on the citrus farms near Clanwilliam.

She sits on the bare earth with her legs crossed and her
blue school skirt tucked tight beneath her legs –

in case her father should ever come back.

He Does Not Know

He does not know what he is doing,
or why he is doing it.

Why it is so early where he is
and so late where he is not.

Why the sky, where he is, is so big
and so limited at the same time.

Why there are so many mountains,
or why there are any mountains at all.

He does not know the answers
to any of the questions anymore.

He is no longer able to think
of even the simplest things:

where to pay for water, for example,
or how to buy time.

III

There

I Carry a Geography

~ Calgary

for Julia

I carry a geography of the dark
with me across oceans, frozen lakes,
mountains whiter than ice, where wind
contours a need urgent as flesh.
This dark, the dark I know,
that does not ever, even in the glare
of dreaming, leave me, this recognition,
familiar and strange as any echo
returning white across a frozen sea,
this dark is you – as long as you,
like the dark, carry absence
in the shape I carry with me.
Everywhere. The geography of a heart
in two halves.

Canadian Geese

The mountains on the far side
of the day are pale and flat.

The college carpark completely
is concreted in white.

Two large and grey geese
drag wings across the steel sky.

Wind makes the sign for waving
from a long cold train.

Tired trees hand an infinitesimal
handful of breath back to gravity.

Silverton

~ New South Wales

The ravens have arrived
out of the sun carrying
sharp flakes in their cries.

The gum trees stand
with their mouths wide open.
An old church sweats.

The sand has been
too long lying out where
no shadow ever passes.

Even metal here feels,
blanched red. The flies
have evolved long fingers

to filch the wind.

Eucalyptus Trees

~ Canberra

Blue sky hidden inside
    old trees.

       Thin branches
exchange movement
    for light.

       The weight
of standing in one
    place pressing,
       pressed

into the red earth.

Ystervarkvallei – I

~ *Makhanda*

for R. B.

Tassel of trees on the fringe of a hill.

     Ridge of blue cicadas.

Concrete column of cloud.

     Fence of moist sunlight.

The tractor of a crow.

     Black muzzle of a fence post.

Small moths substituting a field of yellow.

     White roots without gravity.

One foot transmitting ice.

     The other transmitting infection.

Open and close, open again.

     Silver gate into a paddock.

Ystervarkvallei – II

~ Makhanda

for R. B.

Brown mushrooms in the grass, and tiny yellow flowers,
and dry cow pats, and clumps of dry grass, and small pieces
of stone, and some broken bricks, and scuffed patches of
bare black earth, and a dead branch, and a piece of rotting
wood, and a lump of concrete, and a twisted roll of wire,
and a rusted section of iron railing, and a broken fence post,
and small purple flowers on long thin stalks, and flies, and
cicadas, and the chirping of birds, and a cold wind across
the back of your neck, and a cold wind across your lower
back where your jersey and your trousers fail to meet, and
low grey clouds over the face of the hill, and the hill still,
still, moving slowly in the foreground, beneath the sun, in
the close and distinct detail of tree and bush and grass, but
still and uniform in the background of brown and grey and
shades of anonymous green.

Highveld Hospital

On a winter morning
in the parking lot of a Highveld hospital,
a rusted drum steams.

It is early.

The long corridors are cold and crowded
with figures in blue gowns clutching
plastic bags and folded forms, small
yellow packets with tablets and prescriptions.

None of the patients talk –
or even look at each other.

There is little to say or do, anyway, except
stand and shiver, leaning together,

waiting for hope to make up its mind.

Winelands One-Stop

On his way home along the N1, he stops in the parking lot
of the Winelands One-Stop.
He drags his legs slowly to the Wimpy.
He sits down by the window and orders a Mega cappuccino,
with artificial sweetener instead of sugar.
He opens his leather bag – the one that his ex, and now late,
wife gave to him.
He takes out *Night Sky with Exit Wounds* by Ocean Vuong.
He takes out his notebook – a Croxley JD623 with 192 lined pages.
He takes out his black Bic ballpoint pen – the one with the broken c
He closes his eyes. He puts his left hand over his eyes.
He rubs his tired eyes.
He is listening – not to the sounds of the restaurant
and the high-pitched muzak.
He is listening out for something taking place inside himself.
It is there that all of his life is taking place,
there now inside him – amongst the plastic furniture
and the greasy leftovers and the pink balloons of his soul –
that his real self is to be heard.

Road Trip

~ a haibun, 2016

after Basho

Rosetta / Oliviershoek

1
Slow wings of a heron across the sunrise rowing.

Half a moon in the early sky.

Half a hill balanced on the narrow horizon.

2
Alone, a farmhouse
appears out of the dawn –
a bird's white wing.

Bethlehem / Winburg / Brandfort

3
Scoured by the sun
and the lowing of clouds,
the sky widens a single blue eye
and shrills and shrills
like a cicada.

4

Step into the shade of a rented room. Suddenly you remember the smell of Cobra Brite floor polish that came in a round tin with the smiling yellow face of the sun. Floor polish sweet as insect spray. Doom. For flying insects. Long lasting. The room has an iron-pressed ceiling, white, with inlaid floral designs. There is a black bakelite pull-cord light switch on the ceiling. Without its long cord. An old wire wastepaper basket in the corner. Just like the ones in your classrooms in junior school. By the time you got to high school, the bins were hardened plastic. Orange or dark brown.

The flat metallic chime of the town's church clock. And through the open French windows comes the sharp smell of creosote from the newly-painted garden fence. The inlaid oval mirror in the centre of the stinkwood wardrobe reminds you of the heavy wardrobe in the corner of your Oupa's bedroom. The wardrobe that held his khaki daywear, and his black Sunday suit with the waistcoat, and the small fob watch on its silver chain. A banana tree rustles and crackles in the wind in the dark garden.

And suddenly you are walking down an avenue of cypress trees that line the entrance of the old part of the town cemetery. There is a flaking sandstone cross on the grave of a little child who died at the age of eleven months and fourteen days in the year 1887. The name of the child has chipped off. There is a rusted iron cross that marks the grave of an unknown British soldier killed in action on 29 June 1899 on Koppieskraal just outside town. Just then a flock of small kestrels takes off into the darkening evening as you walk down the avenue of old cypress trees back to your room.

5

Phathakahle ("Handle with care") township. Number 802, the small dilapidated house where Winnie Madikizela Mandela was placed under house arrest in 1977 for almost ten years.

Trompsburg / Philippolis / Colesberg

6

Brown sugar in heaps.
The hills are poured across the plain.

7

An old wheelchair under a tree outside an abandoned house.

Two horses standing nose to tail.

A rusted bakkie dragging a sack of dust down the road behind it.

Norvalspont / Burgersdorp / Hofmeyr

8

You drive back, through the white veld, from viewing the monument to the women and the children who died in the concentration camp at Norval's Pont between 1901 and 1902, back along the bumpy dirt track to the turn-off onto the freeway, with the brown information board and its cluster of white crosses. It occurs to you that returning from a particular destination is always shorter and quicker than the journey outwards. From this thought flows another one. That the dead, all the dead, are perpetually stuck on a road toward their destination, and that is why they seem to be taking so long, why they are so long absent and silent. While the living are always the ones returning – always on the quicker road back, which is why they are always here and now, always with us, hardly gone, hardly missed. But, of course, this begs the question: what is this destination that the dead are always travelling to, and never seem to reach, while the living race back from it in the blink of an eye? Is it perhaps (in a paradoxical way) death itself, the moment of death, that we, the living, are rushing from – not realising, in fact, that the quicker the journey, the sooner we arrive at our own death. While those who are dead are, in fact, so far away from death; so long is the road that they are travelling towards death that they will actually never arrive. And therefore they cannot die, because they are so deeply dead already. And this difference – this paradoxical movement towards something that is, in fact, already behind us, and away from something that is still ahead – this difference accounts for the absolute gulf between the living and the dead. For the terrible separation that is also at the same time almost like a memory. A memory and a forgetting at the same time. The way an amputee remembers and forgets his missing limb.

9
In the deep armchair, you sit
with the shaded lamp on one side,
the wind on the other.

When the wind blows the light
across the room
and back,

you have to grip the arms
of the chair to stop yourself
pitching overboard.

Cradock / Bedford / Port Alfred

10

The monument to the Cradock Four – Matthew Goniwe, Sparrow Mkhonto, Fort Calata and Sicelo Mhlauli – kidnapped and murdered by the South African security police on 27 June 1985. Four gigantic concrete pillars. The adjacent information centre has been vandalised. Windows broken. Doors smashed. Electric cables ripped out of the walls. Roof sheets ripped off. Weeds and long grass and broken glass and faded election posters bearing the face of Jacob Zuma.

11

The fishermen the seagulls the mist low over the surface of the sea the skin of the cold crawling with wind the stones the feathers the sand-clogged waves the fishermen again the dead shark its gaping mouth the gulls wheeling the gulls screeching and women laughing and bent backs and rain suits with arms and long wet knives and blood the blood and men laughing the wind again the low moan of the sea.

Hamburg / Fraser's Camp / Makhanda

12

A man in blue overalls. Blind in one eye. A chainsaw in his hand.

A woman in a blue dress. Head shaved. White clay on her face.

A young girl in a faded school uniform. Tie around her head. Hand on her hip. Hitch-hiking.

An old man in a wheelchair. Thin legs sticking out of his pyjama trousers.

A yellow dog. Tied up with wire. To a gatepost without any fence.

Alice / Hogsback

13
Sharp cries in the forest.

The hoarse creak of a crow's beak.

Wind hard as water eroding sunlight.

14
One hand cannot feel.

The other cannot see.

And the wooden one doesn't know where everyone is anymore.

IV

Mother

The Dripping

There is a dripping in my head.

> Mother says she was always
> the largest girl in her class at school.

A flock of sacred ibises erupt from a tree.

The neighbour hoots for his wife to come
and open the motor gate for him.

Someone has turned off the water at the mains in the street again.

> Mother says the only thing she ever won at school
> was the St John's Ambulance badge for best bandage technique.

The wind has died down and the fires on the hillside
at last are out.

I can see the thin blue sky again.

There is a dripping in my head.

> Mother left school in standard five to work in her parent's
> fish and chip shop at the end of west beach in Port Alfred.

Those are not clouds anymore.

Those are no longer trees.

Someone has pulled out the plug from the bottom of the ocean
and I am being sucked into the current.

Mother says she was an only child
and both her parents were adopted.

My pockets are filling up with syringes and sand.

My pockets are filling up with surgical masks.

I have to write something, anything, anything,
just so as not to hear   the dripping in my head.

The House

At the bottom of his glass is a small house with a small
mother inside.

The house has green walls and a green roof too, and there
are buckets inside the ceiling for loneliness.

The small mother is heavy and bent over an aluminium walker
that goes ahead of her everywhere she goes.

The small house and the small mother get smaller the further
he moves his glass away.

The small house and the small mother have water inside
every part of them that is not sealed with packing tape.

At the bottom of his glass is a sealed cardboard box
with the scent of orange blossom and jasmine.

But he is unable to swallow anything anymore.

Neither birds with long beaks nor salt, neither the seed-pod
of a plane tree nor the scent of regret.

For the small house is dissolving.

Now he feels something irrefutable sear the back of his throat.

Dear Letter

for Mother

1
I am writing to tell you
that the burning
has begun.

2
Although it is cold at night,
the lemon tree
outside the kitchen door
already has white blossoms.

3
Coming back on the freeway
from seeing you yesterday
(after how long?),
I drove over a small buck.

4
Even with all the windows shut,
smoke from the cane fires
filled the inside of my car.

5
And then it struck me
that you were a stranger
stranded inside an old woman's skin
and not my mother anymore.

6
The small buck on the freeway
was already dead.
But that did not stop it
making a sound
against the undercarriage.

7
The echo of something
that long ago
had stopped happening.

8
It is that time of the year.
The burning has begun.

9
All the animals are fleeing.

10
Your eyes
your eyes
your eyes
oh, Mother!

11
Filled with so much smoke.

V

Everywhere

Old Chairs

The old chairs move by themselves at night
in the lounge when the little snakes come out.
They cannot get comfortable on the cold tiles
no matter what position they sit or stand in.

The old chairs stopped dreaming long ago of ever
going back to the warm ocean and summer thunder storms.
They barely make a sound when the carcasses
of dead birds appear overnight in their laps.

The old chairs have resigned themselves to the smell
of animal fur, and to cold nights on their own without dreams.
They have resigned themselves to dying
far from the white sand where their umbilical cords are buried.

The Figure

I wake up at night to a figure hunched
in the glass wings of an antique dressing table.

The figure dreams of melted stones and shadows
sticky with sweat; it has no eyes,
this thing that moves contrary to its desire,
only dark holes where drawings of words once were.

The figure waves a swarm of flies away
from its incurable mouth, as an old wind twitches
a curtain across its memory of tongues
licking salt from each other's thirst.

The figure moves its big head slowly,
the way some ancient stone might if it could.
For there is not much difference between
the living and the never-lived.

In the glass wings of the antique dressing table,
the figure dreams of speechlessness:
the acquiescence of skin to salt and fire.

The Door

The old door –
door with the tarnished brass knob.

The heavy door –
door with the pile of dead leaves
     banked up against it.

The solid door –
door with the four large bolts
     drilled into the front
     on top and on the bottom.

The serious door –
door with the painted flat face
     and long brown streaks
     of rust running down
     from the top to the bottom.

The speechless door –
door with the reputation for
     obscene thoughts and a curiosity
     about the secrets that bricks carry,
     facing day and night, inside and out,
     at the same time.

The skinless door –
door with an insatiable desire for dressing up in human attributes.

The Tongue

Tongue with broken wings.

Tongue without electricity. Because the men in hard hats
are unable to repair last night's storm damage.

Tongue that likes biting itself. Likes chaffing across a broken molar
at the bottom on the left where lying begins.

Tongue with an overcast sky on the outside. Four ibises
in a slow paddling row.

Ocean in the place of his bed.

Tongue by the morning swollen from licking salt
off the bed-sheet.

Tongue in the brown tweed jacket inherited from his grandfather.
Cigarette burn on the left sleeve.

Tongue at the opposite end of his hands. The end where
his heart should be.

The Old Man and the Dead Man

And the old man stumbles backward in his bathroom.

And he grabs onto the basin to stop himself falling.

And he looks down.

And the silent floor is suddenly so far below him.

And at the same time in the thick forest, a cuckoo sings.

And at the same time in the thick forest, a dead man records
the darkness with his cell-phone.

And the dead man records the cuckoo singing in the forest.

And two little boys walk up a steep hill carrying their father's ashes.

And the old man in the bathroom scoops his dirty water into a bucket.

And he looks down.

And he sees that there are large drops of blood on the silent floor.

And he pretends that the drops come from someone else, from
the dead man perhaps.

And in the thick forest, the wife of the dead man tears her clothes.

And the wife of the dead man shaves all her hair off.

And that is how, that is how the old man in the bathroom comes
to understand that he does not feel anything anymore.

Naming

~ in memoriam: Michael Wessels (1958–2018)

It is still dark.
No birds are singing, though the night is almost over.
Only a few roosters crow in the village.
And an engine close by beats its low bass.
There is a hole somewhere. I can feel it.
Something is missing from the order of the world.
Everything I touch feels as if it could shatter or crumble.
The earth is tilted, and I am sliding.
My hands don't know what to do anymore
when they try to pronounce the usual words.
Like flower, tree, mountain.
Like river, rock, woman.
I can feel it the way an amputee still feels his arm.
The arm he used to hold his children –
to hold his wife.
And this absence, this presence of sharp loss,
has a name and a face.
I must name it so that I can stand
even though the earth is tilted:
the name of this absence is your name;
the face of this absence, your face.

Filing Cabinet

~ after 'Metal Cabinet, Laundry' by Andries Gouws

And still the room moves
and the metal filing cabinet too
and the shadow where the tiled floor
and the corner of the metal filing cabinet
and all their respective angles come together

And still the electric tension
and the light holding its breath
and all thought also still suspended
and alone as the short black power cord
and the small electric socket suspended too

And yet still nevertheless and even because
and subject to time and subject to light
and the sharp diagram of silence
and the shadow's inevitable
and the light's as well
slow then still
decay

VI

Bone

Old Bone

On a sheep's knuckle-bone
all day he gnaws,

cold in the furthest of his feeling.

White and wet, the hours melt
'til only the wind's dull beat

on the skin of sky remains,

and three blackbirds in a row,
three smudges he struggles

to separate from their sound.

Breath of an old bone,
breath of the slow bone

brings all of his old words forth.

VII

Nowhere

How Now

How now in winter so quiet

the days go; the light only

thin, insubstantial as if

just tracing paper between;

and the mountains so still

too, the way nakedness

makes us all; no sudden

movements; no loud

sounds; wind and the trees as

if all underwater; yes; eyes

open; holding their breath.

Wall

The wind comes in the night
        when everybody is asleep,
and builds a wall
        between the sky and gravity.

When we wake and walk
        in the forest of tall gum-trees,
smelling the eucalyptus and the
        wet earth, we do not notice

how much the sound of leaves
        is like bricks tossed
up to the second storey –
        where the loud light lives.

Who

Who is the one who opens and closes the heavy gate
so that the fully laden truck can drive through
and out the other side?

Who is this person whose job it is to step out
into the heat barefoot, to grasp the hot metal of the gate
and heave it open and then close it again?

Who is this person? Tell me.
Is it the one who sits in the back?
Is it the one who always sits behind?

The one who always has to
peer between the shoulders of everyone else
in order to see the world.

Design

A cold wind blows
up from the belly of his bones.

He is the fist
thrust firmly into his own mouth.

He is the blindness
hobbling his breath in a public bathroom.

A curtain and a coat
are wrapped around his shivering shadow.

A cross-hatching of rain
cuts emergency signals into his skin.

He grips tighter
and tighter the candle of the corridor.

Inside him are birds,
and outside the waywardness of walls.

The Handle

There is something growing
out of the top of his head.

Like the handle on a pot
or a kettle, it sits there,
joined fast to his skin.

Now he knows why his mother
warned him never to walk under
scaffolding or ladders,
just in case somebody above him
should suddenly pick him up.

Now he knows, too,
why he is so fearful of God.

The Future

The memory of the future
has no smell.

The memory of the future has no hands
either to touch our dreams.

The future just points with its eyes:

give me that!
I want to go there!

Appetite

He ate the first fingers of his melancholy.

Raw. He sucked the nakedness of his regret.

Wet. He lay on his back and licked.

Dry. The bitter leaves of nostalgia.

Seven times. The neck of desire in his hands.

The old. Fruit of sorrow in his gut.

Nothing else. No. Nothing in his life.

Tasted of this. Dry and wet all around.

Taste. Of his own rawness.

Morning Finds Him

Morning finds him
on his knees and hands again.

Wet bandages drying
between his broken teeth.

Branches and small birds
squabble inside his mouth.

He scrabbles in the dirt
like a chicken

for his lost fingerprints.

VIII

Aubade

Aubade

The sky is burned ahead of them.
All the trees have fallen flat.
The moon is late, and is said to be losing.
Wind is predicted for the streetlights.

They might be lying together catching their breath.
They might be dressing silently, filling
their eyes for the long drought ahead.
Or none of these really. Only birds
keening amongst the leaves.

The road is empty ahead of them.
The sidewalks are solitary again. Silence
has the shock of skin sliced through the middle.

Acknowledgements

Thanks are due to the editors of the following journals in whose pages versions of some of these poems first appeared: *New Coin, New Contrast: South African Literary Journal, Illuminations, Prairie Schooner, Scrutiny2, Coming Home: Poems of the Grahamstown Diaspora, Scrivener Creative Review,* and *The McGregor Poetry Festival Anthology 2016* and *2018.*

With thanks to Robert Berold for his inspiration and advice.

And to Dan Wylie for his invaluable comments.

Thank you to Michèle Betty of Dryad Press for her support and professionalism.

Kobus Moolman

Notes on Epigraphs/Quotations

Phrases, epigraphs and quotations have been used, sometimes
with and sometimes without acknowledgement from the following
sources:

Page 1

*There is a moment, in the mountains, when the first light does not so
much fill the sky as empty it still further, the day itself initiated by a
vacuum opening in the east.*

Stephen Watson *A Writer's Diary* (Cape Town: Queillerie
Publishers, 1997)

Page 1

In essence, the poet has only one theme: his live body.

George Seferis *A Poet's Journal: Days of 1945–1951*, trans. Athan
Anagnostopoulos (Cambridge, Mass.: Harvard University Press,
1974)

OTHER WORKS IN THE DRYAD PRESS LIVING POETS SERIES

AVAILABLE NOW

In Praise of Hotel Rooms, Fiona Zerbst
catalien, Oliver Findlay Price
Allegories of the Everyday, Brian Walter
Otherwise Occupied, Sally Ann Murray
Landscapes of Light and Loss, Stephen Symons
An Unobtrusive Vice, Tony Ullyatt
A Private Audience, Beverly Rycroft
Metaphysical Balm, Michèle Betty

OTHER WORKS BY DRYAD PRESS (PTY) LTD

missing, Beverly Rycroft
The Coroner's Wife: Poems in Translation, Joan Hambidge
Unearthed: A Selection of the Best Poems of 2016,
edited by Joan Hambidge and Michèle Betty

Available in South Africa from better bookstores, internationally from
African Books Collective (www.africanbookscollective.com)
and online at www.dryadpress.co.za

People! Read Poetry

Printed in the United States
By Bookmasters